Cindy!
Happy Birthday! [illegible]
Love Flows [illegible]
all each day always...
throughout life.
Enjoy!
Love Patricia

Depths of Love

Depths of Love

A Poetry Collection

Artricia A. James

VANTAGE PRESS
New York

FIRST EDITION

Published by Vantage Press, Inc.
516 West 34th Street, New York, New York 10001

Manufactured in the United States of America
ISBN: 0-533-11888-3

Library of Congress Catalog Card No.:96-90088

0 9 8 7 6 5 4 3 2 1

Contents

Depths of Love

In the Night

Night's mist
stars so high above shine brighter
than the moon's light.
Above all secret moments are stolen
to share the night's mist
under the stars.
Grasshoppers and crickets rub their
legs to the sound of the coming night;
each jumps to the side of its mate
together they jump away into
the night's mist.
Stars so high above have no one
to share in the precious night, only
to await their departure
for the sun above.
All secret moments are now coming
into the day's light
put to rest for the lonely hours of the day;
for the time chosen for moments
of happiness
will be night, along with the beautiful stars
of the night's mist, bringing the
joyous effect it has in
the night.

Realizing the Mistake

Realization of true happiness
that exists inside
comes to life when close to leaving.
Knowing an important being
in one's future lets itself be known
after the tragic mistake has been made.
Nothing can be done to change
that which was or that which will be.
Feelings and fears are at hand;
no one is to take the blame,
the guilt to be shared equally
by all known to the fact of this precious loss.
Bring forth into the light of day
where the matter can be analyzed;
realization of grave mistakes
is not always there
when the situation calls,
only when the situation is headed . . .
for disaster.

Hope for Love

Our love so special and strong, gave me hope
of being loved.
In so many ways, I have tried.
To be honest, loving, and true
is right. . . .
Inside the need to be needed grows more.
From our love have come many great things,
the strength I hold, feelings, trust and warmth,
things that touch the heart in special ways.
Our love was made in heaven to be
more than a natural love.

Looking Back

The days ahead frighten me
in many ways;
much will be slipping away.
Away from my reach
things I could not prevent.
In one day, one year will vanish
in a few words.
In days past, I have remembered
the glow in your eyes, the passion inside,
the soft touch of your hand.
This and more will leave for me
to be with my thoughts of you.
The days ahead are filled with much
loneliness and space.
Maybe another day and time,
experiences will come to pass
in exchange for a better day.

Run to Love

With my heart I fully love you
(the reasons why I do not know)
in many ways known to a woman that
she can love.
When there is a man to accept,
there will be no time or place for this love to be.
Let your love for me show as
mine for you.
To run will put it off
only for a while.
When you can run no more, my love will be;
come to me now,
together we can run . . .
to love as one.
There will be no chains, only promises made
to hold what we have together.
Reasons why may now come
though the answers may not.

I Love You More

I love you more
than the words I speak
say I do.
From the first glance I knew
you were meant to be.
From the glow in your eyes,
the sparkle of your smile,
all linger in my mind a
long, long while.
My heart misses you, my body wants you,
my mind needs what you give
away, there is no excitement to be found.
Here each day is like the
first kiss.
It may be gone soon; let me
love you a while longer.
Time does not promise me love.
You can promise love and more.
I love you more under the star's light
caressing each part of you,
finding the love inside
to hold
always.

Escape for Two

You and I together, in a place
all our own
—outside this place is the world
from which we can escape—
a place all our own to chill and fill
with times only we know of.
Inside away from all we know is our world.
Ours alone, which exists for no other;
time will not reveal.
Happy days and precious nights spent in a world made of
you and me.
Together we make our world better than real,
worth the time.
A place built for escaping
into a world others only dream of,
love-making here is not a must, but a yes;
coming in to be in this world
special feelings and memories are held here,
each time to bring more and more life
to light.
Like the tree waiting for the morning's light,
here everything is perfect as perfect can be.
The agony of facing another hard day
is gone.
The days ahead are wonderful
and peaceful—
listening to the wind blowing through the trees,
walking hand in hand through our woods,
smelling the fresh pine in the air,
nothing in this world can compare
with the rightness of this land of ours.

The Loneliness Time

The words were so sweet.
Now like a spoiled child;
more and more is wanted. Though they
were once so special to me,
now have no true meaning.
Trying to hold on alone is rough
when the pain is so great.
Time heals all wounds,
at a day set aside.
Wounds open
each time I hear your name.
Haunting memories return, with them
the desire to be alone.
Loneliness is the time in which
one realizes mistakes made in life.
Why now?
Everything was so right, being with you
Accepting the loss is hard
after hearing the sweet words
once whispered to me.

I'll Wait For You

By chance we have come together to build
a fantasy into reality.
Dreams of you are now to end
in the arms of another.
You did not belong
away from my reach and sight.
This was tough to see.
At this time and place we were
meant to be.
Surroundings did not permit our bond to seal—
the crack was there for another. . . .
Separation is unbearable,
when you are in her arms.
Looking into your eyes, brings tears
to mine,
for I know that you were meant for me.
With me I would give happiness and love
and all the warmth you needed to be
stably satisfied.
There is the knowing
you want me as I you
to give all that is within ourselves
to make ours better than the rest.
In the present it may never be,
but inside you will know that it was I
who wanted you for my own
to hold, kiss, and love
at your side.
In my heart I believe we were
meant for each other. Waiting
is a slow but meaningful process;

not to wait or worry anymore
is the reward.
One day you will be mine
openly, fully, and honestly.
My arms wait
for the day that I will have the chance
to prove freely that
I've wanted you for my own.

That's What You Mean to Me

I love you with all my heart.
In ways that are real and seem special.
There are no words that
could say what you mean to me.
Others believe that it is untrue
that I believe what is felt in my heart.
Words could not touch you in a way to understand;
they would only give an idea of the questions
you once thought.
Each day the loneliness grows
into an ecstatic need to have you by my side.
Strangers we could never be
unless. . . .
Hard to believe the days
I try not to remember.
Pain is only the result;
I love you with all my heart and
by me you shall never know
(never).
To know would make all the effort we've put forth
slowly fade away.
Inability to bring back a love such as mine
is demanding,
may put a weight upon you.
In a special part of your heart, save a space for
the love I bring to you.

Cherish what it means,
for I love you with all my heart.
I do love you, believe and understand.
I love you as the man
you are to me.
This is to be believed.

Eyes of Decision

The eyes of decision roll in your head
alone to roll the straight or hard
path of loneliness.
Eyes roll the paths to seek
the realness of all things
and persons of life.
Roll through the paths and the journeys
the days will take you
through to learn each new
day of experience.
Take the challenge and love it;
taste the flavor of adventure
and decisions that follow or come with.
The eyes of decision roll in
your head as you will let them
to go to the depths involved
in the making of lifelong decisions.

For You

For you I write this poem.
Each thought I hold reflects
a part of you.
To hold a thought is safer than you.
Things were meant to be shared by two.
Fun does not come to one alone.
Each day I face is hard alone,
Though with you days could fly.
I would give you my love,
Hoping to have yours in return.
Only this once have I chanced a dream;
You are my dream.
I could be much more
With you.
In ways I am not what you want.
Though I would try rather than not care.
I write this for you.

Woman

She is more precious than jewels—
nothing you desire can compare
with her.
Long life is in her right hand;
in her left hand are riches and honor.
Her ways are ways of pleasure.
All her paths are peace.
She is a tree of life to those who lay hold of her,
those who hold her fast are called happy.

A Feeling Is . . .

A feeling for me is there.
Together, close to each other,
we will never be.
The unforgettable kisses, tender ways of
the love we made, will never be.
A force is in the way . . .
blocking . . .
It matters not what happens
for a long time
between lovers.
Still a flicker to help the flame glow.
Not ready to be all alone.
The facts cannot be faced.
They do not fit,
for those who do not understand.

Lovers

A man and a woman
strangers from different worlds
both searching
for something rare and beautiful—
in each other's arms it is found.
The rare beauty of each other
pleasurable security in the arms of two strangers.
A man and a woman
with the same needs found
innocently and rare.

Beautiful Dream

Meeting you as I did
a dream.
A dream with you and me,
conversations of friends and others,
your eyes filled with light from the stars.
Your smile perfect
as a man's should be,
your body, a structure of beauty
perfect in every way.
Each minute, each kiss happened
through a dream.
Unbelievable for love to be
between strangers for one night;
never again will we meet.
Cherished . . .
a beautiful dream of one night.

All Hard and Not

Be with me
through all hard and not.
Understand what is happening;
let it all be known to me,
what is felt.
Every step of the way
don't turn away to spare my feelings.
Let me be in the thoughts . . .
the ones that travel through your mind.
Feel with me it is safe.
Hard as things may get
stay and share each one
with me.
Together through all hard and not
we will make it
together.

Secret Passions

Days are fully planned;
time is not enough.
Filled with the words I have for you.
In ways unknown this is the right way.
Take the time, explore, find means to
completely fill . . .
a song frequently plays over and over.
Each verse new, wanting to be discovered
through the past; we don't know what we
want.
Escape from truth and reality;
leave pain of love behind as soft
as a petal's touch, there will be
a day full.
Time for this was never meant to be;
problems and friends made it known,
among the few—
what time wants to do.
Apart the days pass like death itself,
together like the breeze against the trees
days are planned, for a time of
you and me.

Grow to Patience

I want to be all right;
at times things seem to be all wrong,
but I'll be all right.
Decisions for change must be made for
things to look up.
Time passes slowly, and with it
are harsh moments.
Events of life are meant to be
cherished and forgotten. . . .
I want to be all right
no purpose will they serve hung
onto.
Answers come from the days of history;
strength to move ahead is there; only a
mind is needed.
Choices I face each day make it hard
to understand why?
I want to be all right;
to snap open would not to be hard to accept . . .
For soon this will be of fact
that time grows great and
with it decisions of life.

Honestly Love

My love for you will always grow.
Always have I wanted you; to love what I hold seems selfish.
I love you more than the stars above.
Wanting you more in a day's time;
in time we will be as one.
No chains nor this to keep us apart;
deep in your heart
I'm there.
As you are in mine;
what's felt now is untrue; the bond will always be, not a sight of you.
Seeing is worth having under my shell . . .
in your eyes I can tell
we are still in growth.
We shall always be in love
to grow and grow.
Love me today and tomorrow
until there is no tomorrow.

Return to Love

Being back again
like a flower blooming over again,
all is forgiven and forgotten—
why now?
The time has come for something better
the first bloom tried but dried up.
A new season. . .
a better time with a fuller bloom.
Together for just one night
proves a lot.
The love is there, also the perfect elements;
maybe this time the sun will shine
deeper and this plant will bloom . . .
To make a better garden.

Obstacle to Love

These days are filled
with dreams of happiness. . . .
Some say the good things are worth
waiting for,
waiting for days, weeks, months, years
are awfully long periods for
a wait.
Preserving the moments are tempting;
they must pass—
the decisions, sometimes hard to make.
Walls are at each turn—
up is a high place to reach though
many try.
Only a few succeed;
dreams of happiness are hard to make real.
The forces are always on the other side
of the fence.
Very hard will I succeed to make
the wall crumble.

Once upon Love

Once upon a great chance
in life there's that special someone.
Someone who will make the clouds
go away.
Someone to have and to hold in days
when clouds tend to stay.
Once upon a secret hope
the special dreams and wishes of
this one
will be this special someone to light
the days and share the night.
Each moment from day to day
every hour from week to week
it grows.
All parts of this need are slowly
remembered in the depths of one's mind.
Details of every moment spent.
To be stored for safe keeping.
Once upon this chance will this happen
meaning much to a certain
someone
who makes these months
extraordinary in more ways than one.
Forever will the beauty be kept.

Door to You

I think of you all the while,
and miss the cuteness of your smile.
Each day I wake to see part of you with me.
Together we are one—apart as two,
before, life was dull with no certain meaning—
we grew close as one;
slightly afraid
you pushed me away.
A wall was always there, I wanted a door
to you for me.
Now your wall is still there, the door
I once looked for has no chance
of being. . . .
I know of no way to open it;
I'll always think of you in the day,
and miss you while away.

A Dream of Two

A dream of two
cherishing each other in the special
moments they had together;
the days were like a diamond heaven,
the nights like a clock
slowly ticking away.
Each second held,
was like
a never-ending paradise.
Words perfectly spoken,
kisses perfectly placed,
the two, a dream,
which was never meant to be.
Trying to hold a dream is like
reaching for a star.
It will never be
a dream of two.
What could have been shared—
more than giving what's
not wanted, real and special
truly a fantasy.

Hidden Fear

I want to hold you close to me
forever and ever.
There shall be no words of happiness nor grief.
The past months alone
the world has changed, my life with it.
Nothing of concern or want
living to destroy.
So badly I have wanted you,
my feelings are there, though we hide
to keep them from exposure.
Fear is in the heart,
fear of love and being loved,
fear of life and the pain.
I need to have you as mine
to share, and show
all that I hold.

You

It was you.
From the moment our eyes met
it was you.
From the first words you spoke
it was you.
From the tingle in your touch
it was you.
From our first kiss
it was you.
The first of all things that were
to begin for us.
From the moment I first saw you
I knew you were for me.
It was you from the first day,
something inside awakened and I began
to live once again
because of you.

I Can Think No More

I can think no more of ways to love you;
I can think no more of ways to hold on;
I can think no more of ways to make you love me;
My words seem like rubber;
they make you hurt and in ways shudder.
The love that was once there
is no more.
Another has come to me, as
has woman to you.
What we had was beautiful, though
it can be no more;
my thoughts will travel with you
to no harm only fair wishes.
I can think no more but to say good luck and good-bye.

Finding You

I have found you at last;
through many I had to go,
in search of what I did not know.
One day my search ended—
you came into my light;
many questions became answered,
wounds began to heal
days were pleasing and satisfying.
A lost feeling inside disappeared;
gratitude came from this though some remain
the same.
Loneliness doesn't solve things.
Composition of self through others
makes one false.
True being is like patience and emotions.

With a Man

To be with a man, and to love a man,
the two are not the same.
To be with a man is to
be at his side always
and his only.
To be in love with a man changes things.
Loving him fully and honestly
is the hardest.
Friends are there but for no good reason,
only trying to get a piece
of his love.
Loving him as much as you can
will never compare with
the expressions you give to him.
To be with a man and only this one
can be rather hard
if this was not meant to be;
this changes as the two of you change.
Stay a while to see if it is good,
if he needs you.
To be needed is the best way
to know he cares enough.
Need him in every way and
love him deeply every day.
In love with this man can cause second thoughts;
if the love you feel is real
others do not matter.
All is all in the world of a man—
give him your heart and
trust he is happy.
Love him and stay by his side.

To be with a man and to love him
at once is beautiful
when he feels he is never alone.
Love and stay awhile with this man.

Love

It is being done
You are working in me
I am receiving that which I desire.

Beyond One Night

Happiness brought unto me for one night
is taken away without sheer might.
Kiss me never more, for your touch
I feel no more.
A talk we once had,
only to end leaving me sad.
Cold is your heart as the wind;
forgive me not to finish this to the end.
Hooked on one is never the way
But always two to make the day.
Life does go on maybe alone,
second thoughts to make it at the side;
two heads are better than one,
better for you and then some.

Nobody Does It Better

Nobody does it better
in each and every way you made it
right.
There wasn't much, the little that was there.
Nobody does it better
each time we love better
with the feelings there.
To you none will compare in
the special ways of you.
In each sense it's always a moment
to wonder.
None can compare to your sweetness;
nobody does it better.

Journey into My World

I think of you in all that I do.
I'm in your world to share
with you.
None in my world
all are alone—
Through each day to pass
my words cannot explain.
My world alone
there in it peace and contentedness.
In your world we are one
and free.
Journeys we take, explore steps
both sweet and tender.
I think of you and in your world
when will we end.
Your world will close to me;
return to mine
alone.

Confess Love

At night I want to lie close to you.
Making love with you,
to be as one with you.
Love me tenderly, kiss me sweetly,
never letting go.
My heart always in constant beat
wanting you so dearly in bond
to stay.
Always this way.
I love you more than you'll ever know—
without your love there's no need
to grow.
With each beat my heart continues to flow
for you.

Appreciate the Day

For all these days spent alone
I write these words of life.
The days roll by as by routine;
the birds sing through the trees;
blades of grass weave with the movement of the
wind's heart.
Sunlight is giving more light to the earth
and her children of the garden;
coolly does the wind spray through
a child's hair as he plays
in the sand.
A smile is formed showing
pleasure and satisfaction
of this day.
To see these days can be like
peering up
from the bottom.
All life is strange, nothing explained.
Wonders continue to stare and wonder.
Days of loneliness bring sometimes
contentedness and fright.
Life hurts those who live with it and
hangs above many who don't.

There For You

As beautiful as we are
nothing has changed
the time and days spent alone;
miss you I will
more and more each day.
My love for you could never end—
doubt me not, my love, for I shall
be there when you are down.
As beautiful as we are
nothing has changed
only time.

Moving On

I want to say good-bye.
It's hard when I know
there is still love in my heart.
It's very hard to want so
desperately
but wanting to leave so suddenly.
Forgive me if you can;
this isn't the way things should end.
Maybe a call now and then,
to be in touch.
Friends always, lovers never again.
The spell is over—
you want me in a way that's
overbearing, too tight for an
open love.
What I feel is different;
time and experience have not settled
down with me.
Days will be different without you;
the love of me you know.

Dream Away

All away,
away from the reality and rules,
thoughts flow freely, past mistakes realized,
realized and laughed at.
Away, away from orders, facts and pain,
nothing matters—then again everything.
Dreams and fantasies come to life
to serve the dreamer.
Dream on, and on it goes; and more
is given not to be taken for granted
only as satisfaction.
Filled to the brink of all dreams of pleasure
all away
never to return to rules and mistakes.

Inside

Inside
that's where it's at
the things that make one tick.
Strange feelings for lovable persons of
wonderful being.
Inside
where no one can intrude or explore
to find all of the unknown treasures
that are especially cherished
for their beauty and
what it stands for.
Inside
no questions to seek answers
only comfort and paths to follow;
most of all, wonders and joys are there.

Lying in the Backyard

The shirt upon the line
blowing in the wind,
trees moving with the breeze,
bricks lie soundless upon the grass
as the music plays,
my mind wanders.
Around, around to thoughts
thoughts of my love and the
happiness felt inside.
As I sit and watch the shirt upon the line
my heart loves . . . loves
the feeling is there, it comes and never goes.
I know not why I chose this of
neutral meaning;
in ways they have special meanings.

All You

From the beginning it was you
the days and nights with you
made life special;
there were times when I could think
of only you,
times that brought tears
that were silently shed—
every thought and memory
are of you.
Time draws you near;
thinking back, all things
I feel inside are for you.

Growing Up

This happens to us
in ways to learn.
A child is born
in the days to come;
the child grows and grows
plays and plays;
age has come upon this child;
the child continues to play;
folks say, "You ain't no child no more,"
the child wanting to stay young
in the world;
the world says you must move on;
this child learns and responds to
the world successfully;
the world has nothing to say.

Learning Days

Days of innocence and peace,
every day a new and exciting pleasure,
each high found among the two
exploring, developing outer limits of
communication, reaching and finding
the knowledge of one another together.
Days of innocence played by chance of this day
ignorant of facts shown in the light.
Lies and repeated love messages are created
loving two is hard to create,
different chemistries, fail to blend in
to form one.
Lies will end, so shall
this phase.
Days ahead are awaiting an explorer
of purity and divine love inside to
possess this knowledge.

Private Hold

My love, what I hold will always be
the magic moments
that are in time with life's happenings.
I love you in my world.
Alone.
When I am in your arms the outside world
dies;
there is no other beyond your touch;
whispers of sweet words are more
meaningful from your lips.
What I hold belongs to you
in more ways than one.
As one, we belong to each other to
ripen as a peach.
Kiss my heart with yours, let the flames rise
with the heights of what is awaiting
in the hold.

Believing Love

Our love so special and strong
gave me hope of being loved;
in so many ways I have tried
to be honest, loving and true
is right. . . .
Inside the need to be needed and loved
grows more.
From our love have come many things,
the strength I hold, feelings of trust and warmth.
Things that toughen the heart in special ways;
our love was made in heaven to be
more than a natural love.

Again

Again a song will play;
again the words will break a heart
again and soon the wound will heal;
again this time next spring
she will come back to you
to share again.
Again things will change
though she'll try to feel the same;
your friends will cover and lie
again to see her face, to know
she still cares.
This time she will leave
not to return again;
again and again you will look
upon her face and know
how wrong you were—
she will love you again and again.
Again, a new song will play
asking for another play.

Final Good-bye

I loved you.
I loved you too.
Something is wrong.
What is it?
My heart feels for another.
What happens to me?
You shall find another.
I don't want another.
I don't love you anymore.
I guess it is over?
Yes.
I am sorry (very sorry).
So am I.
This was nice.
Thanks.
Well, this is good-bye?
Yes.
Good-bye.
Good-bye.

Struggle to Love

I love you, yes, I know,
though deep inside, my heart tells me
this isn't so.
Many times have I tried to make this right;
each time I try I feel this is a losing fight.
We have shared much in our time;
I feel I'm in a bind.
It pains me to let you go but,
I can only follow my heart, for it tells me so.
The sparkle in your eyes, the tenderness of your smile,
for me I won't care to see them
for a while.
I love you, yes, I know;
there is no other way for me to go.
Friends say it was wrong to do;
they cannot feel as I did for you.
It will be hard as the days go on
and for you there will be
another song.

Thank You

Thank you for the light;
thank you for the day;
without you there would be no way;
thank you for loving me;
thank you for caring, it was worth the wait.
Thank you for trying once again;
thank you for your tender moments,
the days I'll never forget.
Thank you for the light through the door;
thank you for showing me what
love can do.
Thank you for the night;
thank you for sharing it in my arms;
thank you for a world of many
days filled with light.

How Do I?

How do I tell him the feeling is no more?
How do I tell him I care no more?
How do I tell him our love is through?
Simply.
It is over between me and you.
How do I not break his heart, when I begin to start?
Things have changed, nothing is the same.
There can be no lies, only the hope that
lies in the skies.
How do I say I hurt as much as he
for the loss of leaving him?
How do I tell him I've got to go,
that this is not a show?
How do I tell him he needs me so?
How do I tell him I am gone
like the morning dawn?

Forget Me Not

Good luck in the years
yet to come.
Alone in my world I'll never be
but yet in the friendly part of the matter
my luck travels with you.
Through thick and thin
always remember this message I bring to you,
only a wind of joy to fill your days.
Enjoy each day you have and
forget not what you once shared
the days before.

There Will Never Be Another

Young as I may be
I have loved many but only one matters.
In return my love has been shared once, cared for
and hurt all the same.
I always tried to do what I considered best.
Towards the ends,
pain and disaster were the result of this relationship.
I have never loved another as I do you.
You are my life and real love
all in one.
Though he breaks my heart and dreams
I'll continue to love him always.
It is as though I am helpless to do anything
but continue to give my love to him,
when he knows it's there.
Always deeply inside I will always love him.
There will never be anyone who
could change it.
Only him.

Friends Are Life

Friends are about life,
without them
things seem unreal and
sort of lonely.
To some they only bring
troubles and grief;
friends are a big pain to all—
they know too much
and destroy life and happiness.
Life is made happier with acquaintances.

My Mind's Eye

Each day I live to try
to experience a new path which my mind travels.

Not a Second Thought

As the days pass
yesterday was only a dream;
none will be the same.
Floating along, things work out
good as the days go by without
a second thought.

Without You

Each day is haunted by the many thoughts of you.
Far away are the secret memories I hold,
bringing back times of smiles and wonderful times.
Lonely are the days ahead . . .
though each day my thoughts are with you.
Days are hard to face when there is nothing to look for;
calls are sent no more, than a daisy expecting life.
Special moments together are no more;
a promise made to make up all the hurt you release.
I hold your promise in my heart to the last word;
no one but I will know that this promise will never be kept.
Each day you haunt my life, I wish you were unknown
though otherwise why would this love exist?
Pain and memory, once more would I want you
for myself for treasure and love.

The Feelings Were Real

What I feel for you is real
up front, there seems to be no chance
to fully express all.
None, not even myself. . . .
Can I fully explain why?
Unreal as all may seem it's a following ghost
of every day,
bringing back all of the needs
you fulfilled so.
Without hesitation.
What was felt at one time has
changed for the better
all to be in your favor.
Feelings of now clash,
bringing heartbreaking thoughts
of what you meant to me.
Things now seem wrong
for the right moments.
Selfish and jealous, yes, I know;
the feelings were real.

Beginning

In the beginning
it was plain and lots of fun;
through the days we have shared much.
Enough, there is never enough
to experience.
Innocent as it may seem,
each hour of the day fulfills a need.
More follows each day.
The beginning to a strong and
always satisfied need.
Nothing could ever compare
to the happiness felt.
The beginning was the best.

Wisdom This Day

Wisdom helps as the days go forward.
The persons considered to be
friends make each easier to face.
Possibly knowing how to deal with
each individual in his own way.
Special feelings may be
to make the road a bit easier to handle.
Still wisdom helps;
others mean well by saying
what they mean.
Only if they knew
what was actually happening.
With hidden words of wisdom
behind what they speak.
Gratitude is coming their way
for opening the door a little more.
Soon the door shall be opened enough
to break the way.
All hell in the world is not
ready for this day.
Wisdom will be a small
part of the shock—then again
it could be too much.
The world will be ready
to accept the knowledge
in ways they are about to receive.

Take a Chance

Believe what you will,
trust me if you can.
Forgive at a risk,
forget if you can.
The days we shared, where
the sun always shone;
to be apart is lonely,
together we kept a smile.
I cared for all too much.
Thought I pressured you as such.
What we had will never leave . . .
though you will;
the feelings were so deep, inside I could not keep.
Easy for you to bring such pain,
to go back to life just the same.
Very much you will never know you hurt me so.
Silence is the way, for apart we must stay.
Crowded a life is never fun, special
is it to be needed as one.
As a friend I try to be, how can I when
you feel not for me?
You're always in my thoughts, though
in ways you should not.
Explanations are asked, but performing may be a task.
A person I am to be known,
I try to let what I feel be shown.

The Dilemma

The end came as a bad wave of shock.
No words were available unto me
for what you have brought to me.
All things seemed right as right
could be, each day was perfect.
The days and time shared with you
were unbelievable until the end
of this came.
There is nothing you left for me to say
in more ways than one;
you terribly hurt my heart and
damaged the one's felt for you.
To this day I shall never understand why
you chose to put me through such a
dilemma as you have.
None shall ever know why;
the beginning I cared deeply
for what we planned to share for a while;
now it will go as I once knew it should
have never been.
It should have never been.

Never Again

You were loved with all due
consideration in mind.
Your love only came from
words, not heart-meant ones.
I feel as though you were honest
but not as you were meant to be.
I needed to explain but you
soon proved there was no need.
Instead of sharing togetherness
we shared separation.
I kept trying to bring us
back once again . . .
Only to find a wall blocking
my path.
Strange as it may seem I
feel as though I shall never have
any feelings for you ever.